I0797282

Little People, BIG DREAMS™

RIHANNA

Written by
Maria Isabel Sánchez Vegara

Illustrated by
Niña Mata

Frances Lincoln
Children's Books

On the sunny island of Barbados, surrounded by the sound of waves and calypso music, there lived a little girl named Robyn. But it was with her middle name, Rihanna, that she would one day become a superstar.

Her dad wasn't around much, so Rihanna often had to look after her two brothers while her mom was at work. To keep them smiling, she sang and danced around the house, turning the living room into their own little stage.

School wasn't always easy. Some kids teased Rihanna because her skin was lighter than theirs. But she didn't let their words dim her sparkle. Instead, she started a band with some friends and turned up the volume on her dreams.

Rihanna and her friends were still thinking of a name for their band when they got the chance to perform for an American musician visiting Barbados. He was amazed by Rihanna's powerful voice and vibrant energy.

Soon after, Rihanna was invited to an audition in New York City, far away from her tiny island. She felt nervous, but she sang her heart out for the head of a big music company. Her performance earned her a record deal that same day!

At seventeen, Rihanna burst on to the music scene with a hit, "Pon de Replay." The title means "play it again" in Bajan Creole, her home language. The beat was so catchy, it had everyone dancing, making Rihanna a star almost overnight!

Two years later, Rihanna surprised everyone with an edgy short haircut and a new, bold style. She released "Umbrella," an amazing hit about friends helping each other. Thanks to that song, she won her first Grammy music award.

But all that success didn't come easy. Behind the bright lights were sleepless nights, long hours in the studio, and endless traveling. Rihanna didn't do it for fame or money—she did it because she truly loved music.

Despite years at the top, Rihanna continued to push herself. "Diamonds" wasn't just another hit—it was an anthem about strength and self-belief. The song touched people all over the world, inspiring them to shine in their own way.

But Rihanna wanted to help people shine in real life, too. She started a charity named after her grandparents, Clara and Lionel. For years, she held a big party called the Diamond Ball to raise money for those who need it most.

Her love for color, style, and fairness sparked a big idea. She created a makeup and clothing brand with shades for every skin tone and sizes for every body. She was also the first Black woman to lead a fashion label for a famous luxury company.

While expecting her babies, Rihanna wore sparkly tops and sheer dresses—showing off her bump instead of hiding it. She helped people see that a growing belly is something to celebrate, inspiring mothers to feel confident and proud.

With every step she took, Rihanna—the little girl from Barbados—proved that we all have a diamond inside us, ready to shine bright. All we have to do is look within and see the beauty that was always there.

RIHANNA

(Born 1988)

2005

2007

Robyn Rihanna Fenty was born on the Caribbean island of Barbados. Her dad had a lot of problems and her childhood wasn't easy. Singing and listening to music became her escape. At fifteen, she got a lucky break—the chance to audition for an American record producer, Evan Rogers, who was visiting the island. He agreed to help her record her first ever song. In the summer of 2005, the seventeen-year-old found herself in New York City, singing in front of legendary rapper Jay-Z, head of the Def Jam Recordings record label. He signed her on the spot. Her first two albums did well, but she really became a superstar in 2007, when she changed her style for something edgier. Her song "Umbrella" became one of the year's biggest anthems. Three years later, she became the only female artist in

2023

2025

history to have four Number 1 singles on the U.S. Billboard charts in a single year. In 2012, Rihanna set up the Clara Lionel Foundation, which works with communities to improve education, healthcare, and more. In her twenties, Rihanna took a break from music and turned her talents to business. Fenty Beauty, her make-up brand, was the first to include foundation for dozens of skin shades. Her clothing line, Savage X Fenty, celebrated women of all shapes and sizes. Rihanna wanted everyone to feel included. In 2023, she made a comeback to the stage at the Super Bowl Halftime show. Her iconic performance revealed a proud baby bump—a second child with rapper A$AP Rocky. One of the bestselling artists of all time, Rihanna is known around the world as a style icon and queen of pop.

Want to find out more about **Rihanna**?

Have a read of this great book:

Rihanna: A Little Golden Book Biography by Regina Andreoni

Original idea of the series by Maria Isabel Sánchez Vegara, published by Alba Editorial, s.l.u.
"Little People, BIG DREAMS" and "Pequeña & Grande" are trademarks of
Alba Editorial S.L.U. and/or Beautifool Couple S.L.
First published in the US in 2026 by Frances Lincoln Children's Books, an imprint of The Quarto Group.
Quarto Boston North Shore, 100 Cummings Center, Suite 265D, Beverly, MA 01915, USA
Tel: +1 978-282-9590 **www.Quarto.com**
EEA Representation, WTS Tax d.o.o., Žanova ulica 3, 4000 Kranj, Slovenia. www.wts-tax.si

ISBN 978-1-80570-175-0
Set in Futura BT.

Published by Juliet Matthews · Edited by Claire Saunders
Designed by Sasha Moxon and Izzy Bowman
Production by Robin Boothroyd
Manufactured in Shanghai, China CC112025
1 3 5 7 9 8 6 4 2

Photographic acknowledgments (pages 28–29, from left to right): 1. Rihanna before the start of the 2005 US Open at the USTA National Tennis Center in Flushing Meadows Corona Park, New York City, on August 27, 2005 © Bryan Bedder/Getty Images. 2. Rihanna performs in Tokyo, Japan, for the Live Earth series of concerts, on July 7, 2007 © Koji Watanabe/Getty Images. 3. Rihanna performs during the Apple Music Super Bowl LVII Halftime Show at State Farm Stadium in Glendale, Arizona, on February 12, 2023 © Kevin Mazur/Getty Images for Roc Nation. 4. Rihanna at the 78th annual Cannes Film Festival at Palais des Festivals in Cannes, France, on May 19, 2025 © Karwai Tang/WireImage.

Collect the *Little People*, **BIG DREAMS**™ series:

FRIDA KAHLO · COCO CHANEL · MAYA ANGELOU · AMELIA EARHART · AGATHA CHRISTIE · MARIE CURIE · ROSA PARKS · AUDREY HEPBURN · EMMELINE PANKHURST

ELLA FITZGERALD · ADA LOVELACE · JANE AUSTEN · GEORGIA O'KEEFFE · HARRIET TUBMAN · ANNE FRANK · MOTHER TERESA · JOSEPHINE BAKER · L. M. MONTGOMERY

JANE GOODALL · SIMONE DE BEAUVOIR · MUHAMMAD ALI · STEPHEN HAWKING · MARIA MONTESSORI · VIVIENNE WESTWOOD · MAHATMA GANDHI · DAVID BOWIE · WILMA RUDOLPH

DOLLY PARTON · BRUCE LEE · RUDOLF NUREYEV · ZAHA HADID · MARY SHELLEY · MARTIN LUTHER KING JR. · DAVID ATTENBOROUGH · ASTRID LINDGREN · EVONNE GOOLAGONG

BOB DYLAN · ALAN TURING · BILLIE JEAN KING · GRETA THUNBERG · JESSE OWENS · JEAN-MICHEL BASQUIAT · ARETHA FRANKLIN · CORAZON AQUINO · PELÉ

ERNEST SHACKLETON · STEVE JOBS · AYRTON SENNA · LOUISE BOURGEOIS · ELTON JOHN · JOHN LENNON · PRINCE · CHARLES DARWIN · CAPTAIN TOM MOORE

HANS CHRISTIAN ANDERSEN · STEVIE WONDER · MEGAN RAPINOE · MARY ANNING · MALALA YOUSAFZAI · ANDY WARHOL · RUPAUL · MICHELLE OBAMA · MINDY KALING

IRIS APFEL · ROSALIND FRANKLIN · RUTH BADER GINSBURG · MARILYN MONROE · KAMALA HARRIS · ALBERT EINSTEIN · CHARLES DICKENS · YOKO ONO · MICHAEL JORDAN

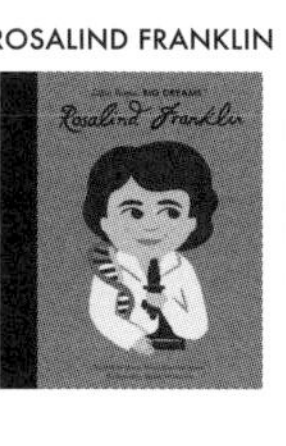

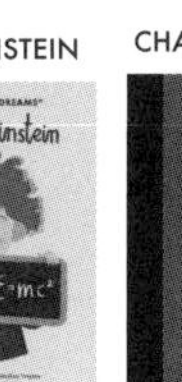

Scan the QR code for free activity sheets, teachers' notes and more information about the series at www.littlepeoplebigdreams.com